KNIGHTS
Activity Book

Winky Adam

DOVER PUBLICATIONS, INC.
Mineola, New York

Note

Have fun as you take a trip back in time to the days when knighthood was in flower. The activities and puzzles in this book will tell you a lot about the life of a knight in the Middle Ages. Find out what it was like to live in your castle, and defend it from invaders. Learn about what you would eat, where you would sleep, and what you would wear. When you have finished the puzzles (or if you get stumped), you can check the answers beginning on page 29.

Bibliographical Note

Knights Activity Book is a new work, first published by Dover Publications, Inc., in 1998.

DOVER *Pictorial Archive* SERIES

This book belongs to the Dover Pictorial Archive Series. You may use the designs and illustrations for graphics and crafts applications, free and without special permission, provided that you include no more than four in the same publication or project. (For permission for additional use, please write to Permissions Department, Dover Publications, Inc., 31 East 2nd Street, Mineola, New York, 11501.)

However, republication or reproduction of any illustration by any other graphic service, whether it be in a book or in any other design resource, is strictly prohibited.

International Standard Book Number: 0-486-40356-4

Manufactured in the United States of America
Dover Publications, Inc., 31 East 2nd Street, Mineola, N.Y. 11501

The First Knights

Over a thousand years ago, Europe was torn apart by civil wars and foreign invasions. Powerful lords recruited warriors on horses to fight for them and to protect their property. These warriors were the first knights.

Hidden in this picture are tools and weapons that were used by knights: a spur, a sword, a battle ax, an arrow, and a mace. Can you find them?

The Middle Ages

Knighthood flourished from A.D. 1000 to A.D. 1400, during the medieval period. This era is often called the Middle Ages.

See how many words you can make from the letters in
MIDDLE AGES.
We have started the list for you.

DIME

SADDLE

Becoming a Knight

A boy trained for many years to become a knight. He learned to behave properly, to look after horses, and to fight. He helped his master dress in armor.

To find out more about preparing to become a knight, read the clues and fill in the crossword puzzle. We've provided the first letter of each answer to help.

Clues

1. A 7-year-old who is sent to a lord's castle to learn manners.
2. A 14-year-old who is apprenticed to a knight to learn how to use weapons.
3. What a young man of 20 receives, when he is deemed ready, with the flat of a sword.
4. What a young man becomes after years of training and service.
5. These were fastened around his ankles to show his new status.

Training

A squire was expected to train hard for tournaments and battles. He practiced with the weapons he would use in war, especially with the sword and the lance.

Sometimes a squire would practice swordsmanship against a wooden post.

Color in the spaces that contain the letter "b" to find out what this post was called.

a	a	a	c	c	c	d	d	d	a	d	d	c	c	c	c	c
d	b	b	b	c	a	b	b	b	b	a	b	d	d	a	a	a
d	b	a	c	b	d	b	c	c	b	a	b	c	c	c	d	d
d	b	a	c	b	d	b	a	a	c	c	b	d	c	d	d	d
d	b	b	b	c	d	b	b	b	a	c	b	d	d	c	a	a
a	b	c	d	c	c	b	a	a	c	c	b	d	d	a	a	a
a	b	c	d	a	a	b	a	c	c	d	b	d	d	c	c	c
a	b	c	c	c	c	b	b	b	b	d	b	b	b	b	b	a
a	a	a	c	d	d	c	c	c	d	d	d	a	a	c	c	c	c

To practice with a lance, a young squire would ride toward a shield which hung on a swinging arm. He had to ride quickly to avoid being hit by the heavy sack at the other end.

Follow the squiggly lines to find out the name of this device. Write the letters in the empty boxes.

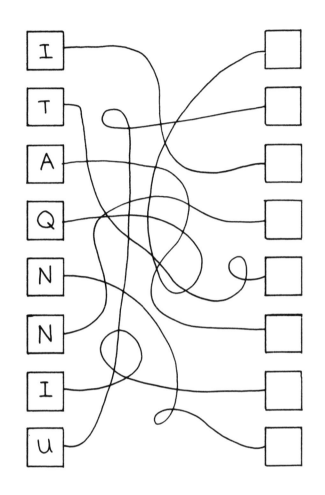

Tournaments

Knights prepared for war by participating in tournaments. They dressed in armor, mounted their horses, and fought each other as teams. While blunted weapons made the tournaments safer than battle, tournaments were still dangerous.

In one type of tournament, two teams tried to knock off the crests of their opponents' helmets. To find the name of this event, use the code to fill in the blanks.

$\overline{3}$ $\overline{12}$ $\overline{21}$ $\overline{2}$ $\overline{20}$ $\overline{15}$ $\overline{21}$ $\overline{18}$ $\overline{14}$ $\overline{5}$ $\overline{25}$

A	B	C	D	E	F	G	H	I	J	K	L	M
1	2	3	4	5	6	7	8	9	10	11	12	13
N	O	P	Q	R	S	T	U	V	W	X	Y	Z
14	15	16	17	18	19	20	21	22	23	24	25	26

To learn the name of the area where the knights fought, read each clue. Write the answers in the boxes. The letters in the dark boxes will spell out the word.

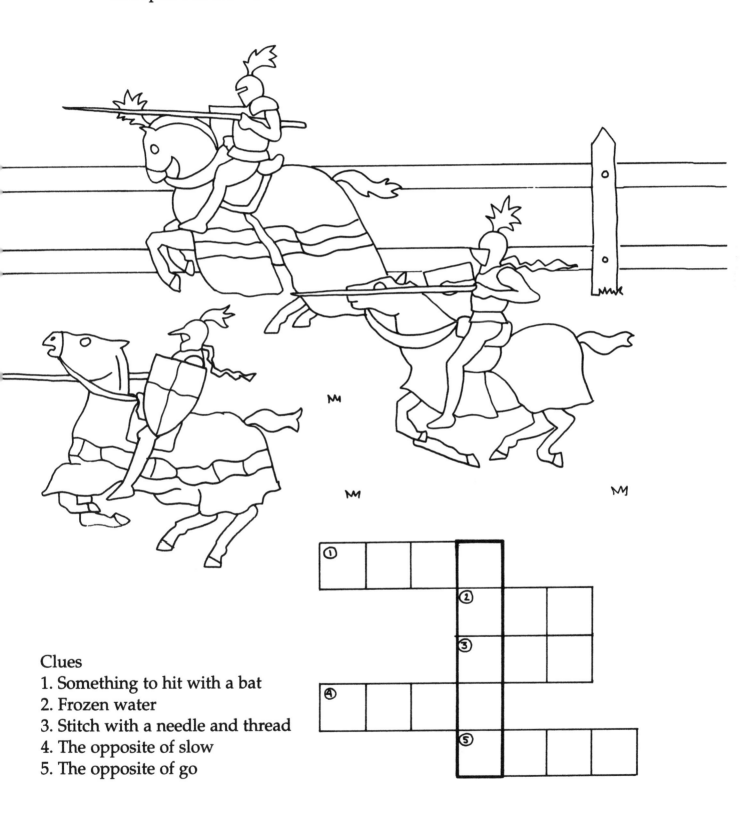

Clues
1. Something to hit with a bat
2. Frozen water
3. Stitch with a needle and thread
4. The opposite of slow
5. The opposite of go

Suit of Armor

Armor protected the medieval knight against heavy blows from the swords and lances of his enemies. Made of many metal sections fastened together, almost every piece of armor had a specific purpose and name.

Look at the picture on the opposite page to see what part of the body each piece was designed to protect. Then, find the words in the puzzle below. The words go up, down, and across.

Pieces of Armor

gauntlet: protects the hand
greave: protects the lower leg
pauldron: protects the arm and shoulder
breastplate: protects the chest
helmet: protects the head
sabaton: protects the foot
gorget: protects the throat
cuisse: protects the thigh
poleyn: protects the knee
cuirass: protects the body

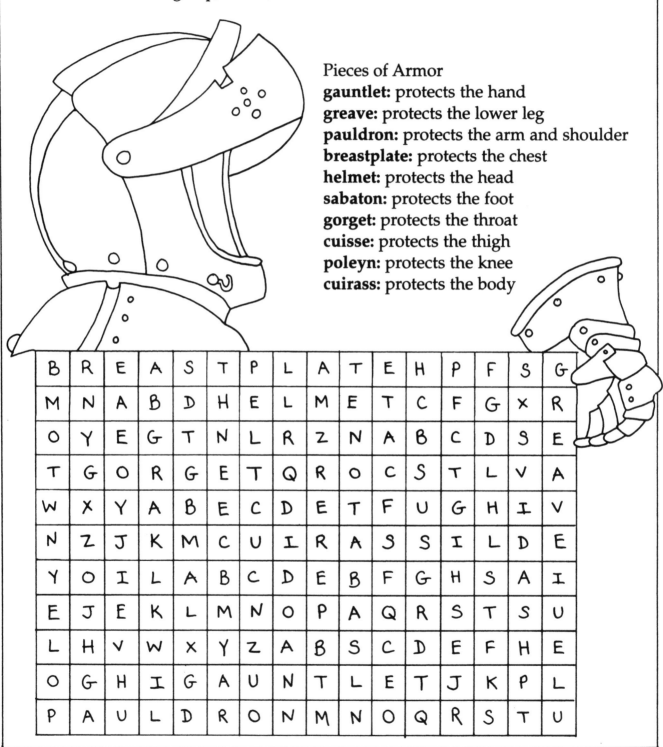

B	R	E	A	S	T	P	L	A	T	E	H	P	F	S	G
M	N	A	B	D	H	E	L	M	E	T	C	F	G	X	R
O	Y	E	G	T	N	L	R	Z	N	A	B	C	D	S	E
T	G	O	R	G	E	T	Q	R	O	C	S	T	L	V	A
W	X	Y	A	B	E	C	D	E	T	F	U	G	H	I	V
N	Z	J	K	M	C	U	I	R	A	S	S	I	L	D	E
Y	O	I	L	A	B	C	D	E	B	F	G	H	S	A	I
E	J	E	K	L	M	N	O	P	A	Q	R	S	T	S	U
L	H	V	W	X	Y	Z	A	B	S	C	D	E	F	H	E
O	G	H	I	G	A	U	N	T	L	E	T	J	K	P	L
P	A	U	L	D	R	O	N	M	N	O	Q	R	S	T	U

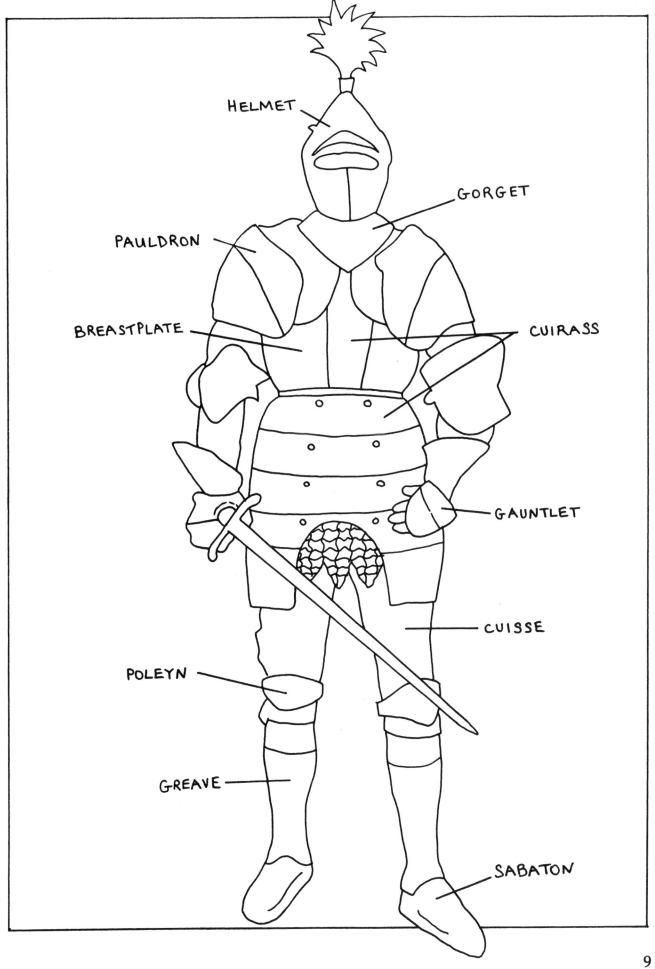

HELMET

GORGET

PAULDRON

BREASTPLATE

CUIRASS

GAUNTLET

CUISSE

POLEYN

GREAVE

SABATON

9

Suit of Armor

These two 16th century knights in armor look the same, but there are 10 ways in which they are different. Can you spot the differences?

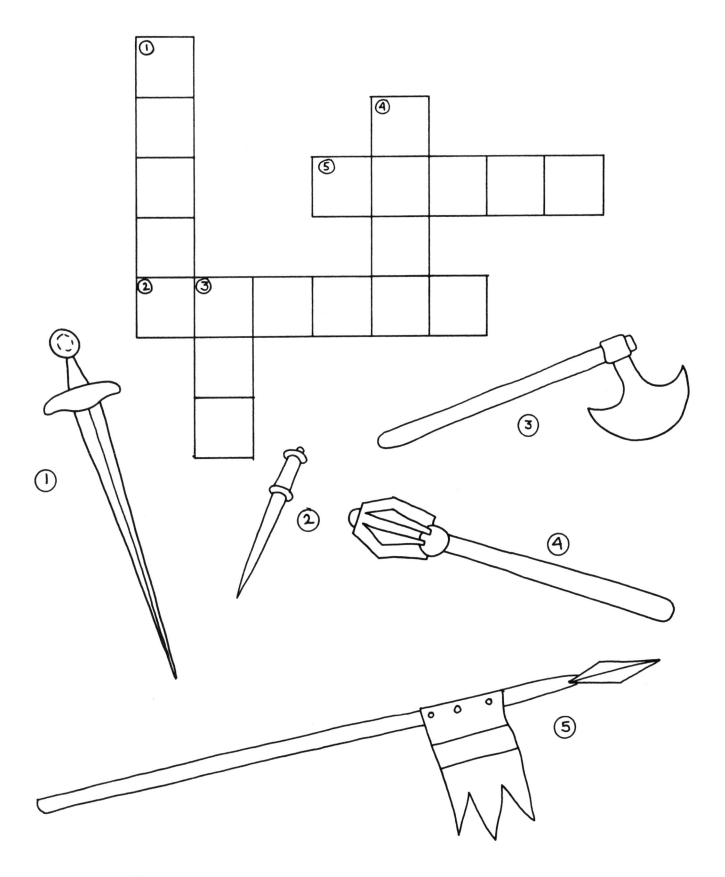

Weapons
Knights had to be well armed. Fill in the crossword to find the
names of weapons a knight might carry into battle.

Horses

Horses were important and expensive parts of a knight's equipment. He had a horse for hunting, a horse for fighting, and a horse for traveling.

Use the code to find the names of horses that would have been owned by a knight.

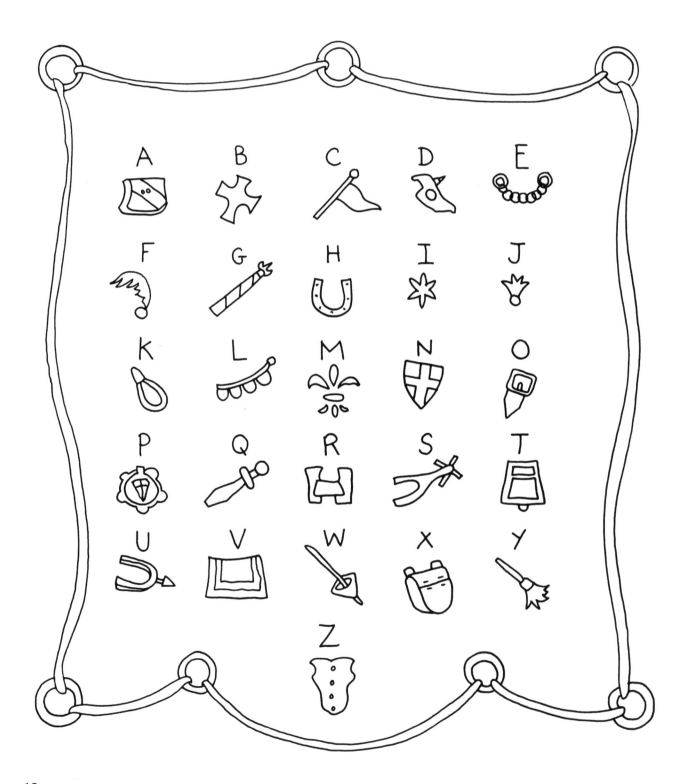

Heraldry

To identify themselves, knights carried shields decorated with boldly shaped, brightly colored symbols. The creation and use of these symbols developed into a system called heraldry. Heraldic symbols were described in a language based on ancient French.

Using the chart, color the shields below.

Color key
or: gold
argent: silver
gules: red
azure: blue
sable: black
vert: green
purpure: purple

background: **gules**
prancing lion: **or**

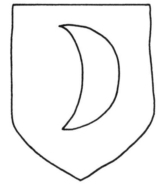

background: **purpure**
crescent: **or**

background: **vert**
cross: **purpure**

background: **sable**
fleur-de-lys (symbol of the French king): **or**

background: **azure**
swimming dolphin: **argent**

background: **azure**
sun in splendor: **or**

Create your own coat of arms here

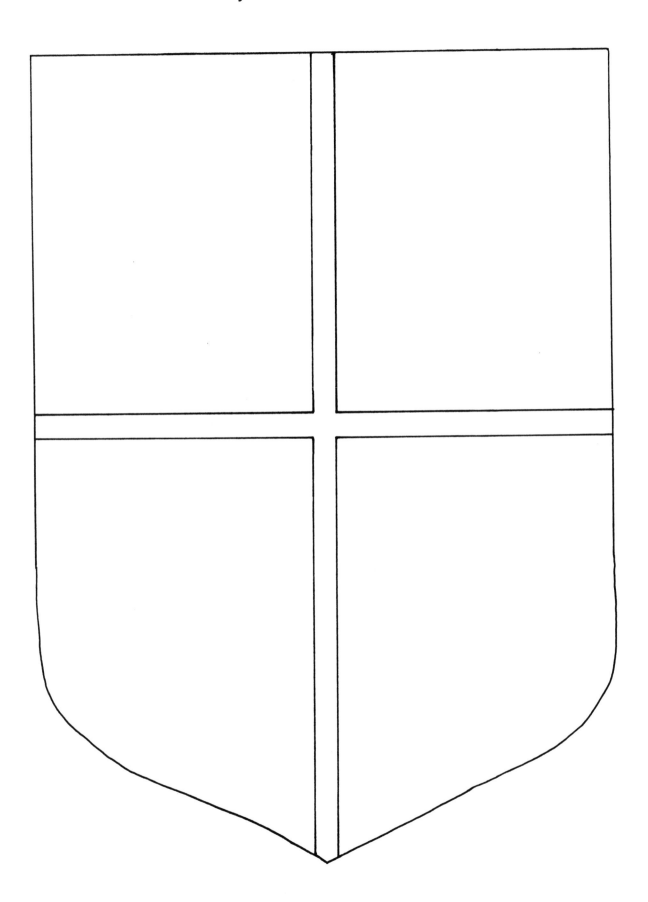

Battle

During wartime, in addition to heavily armored knights on horses, there were also soldiers with crossbows, archers, and pike men on the field of battle.

These pictures have been cut in half. Draw a line from one column to the other to match up the pictures.

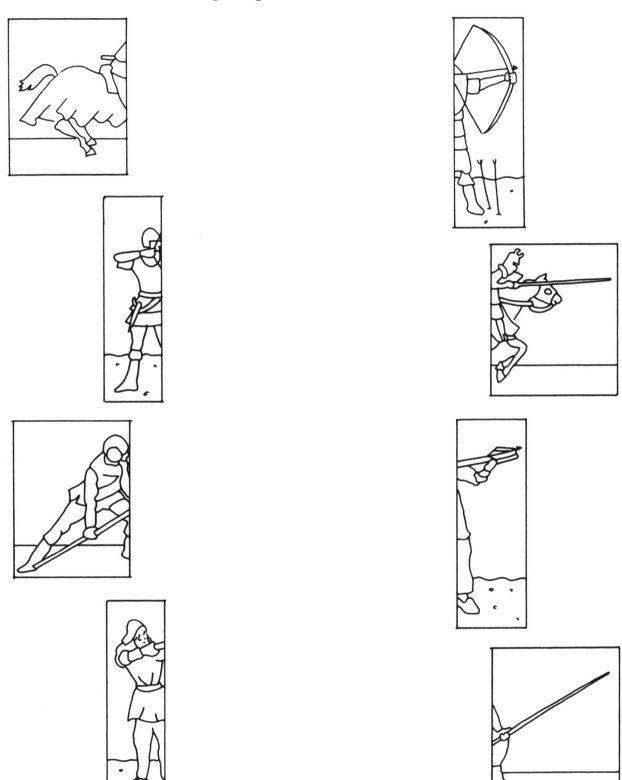

Hunting

Hunting, a favorite sport of knights, provided food for the table. Knights hunted deer, boar, rabbits, and birds, usually with the aid of specially trained falcons and dogs.

Help this rabbit find his way to safety.

Siege Warfare

When an enemy wanted to take control of a castle, he would lay siege to it. By surrounding a castle with soldiers, he would try to drive out the defenders through starvation. A direct attack required special weapons and techniques to help the attacker break through the castle walls.

Here are a variety of weapons and techniques armies used to attack a castle. Find these words in the puzzle. The words run down, across, on the diagonal, and backwards.

catapult: a device used for hurling large stones, spears, and arrows at an enemy

ballista: a giant crossbow for launching rocks

trebuchet: a catapult that worked like a seesaw

mangonel: another kind of catapult

belfry: a wooden tower dragged to a castle wall by invaders during a siege

mining: digging under a wall to gain access to an enemy

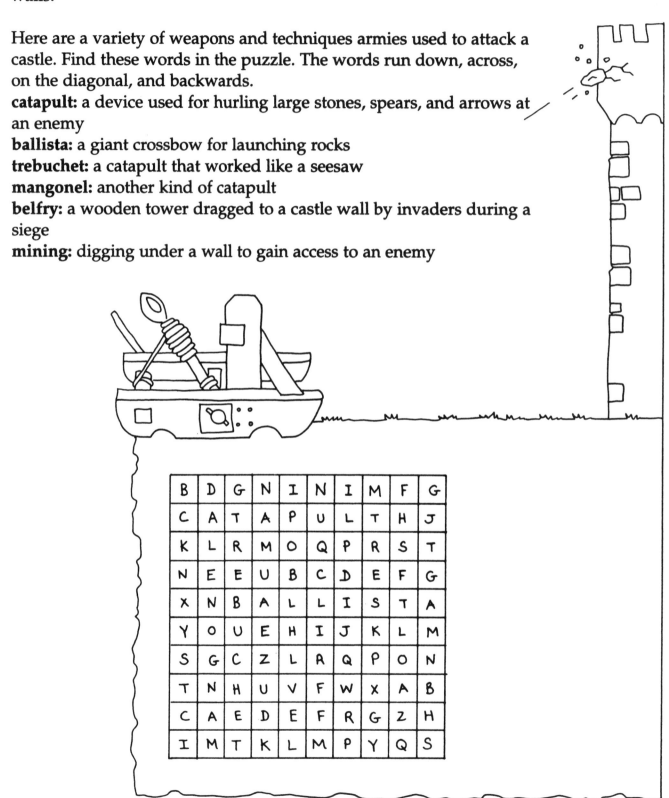

B	D	G	N	I	N	I	M	F	G
C	A	T	A	P	U	L	T	H	J
K	L	R	M	O	Q	P	R	S	T
N	E	E	U	B	C	D	E	F	G
X	N	B	A	L	L	I	S	T	A
Y	O	U	E	H	I	J	K	L	M
S	G	C	Z	L	R	Q	P	O	N
T	N	H	U	V	F	W	X	A	B
C	A	E	D	E	F	R	G	Z	H
I	M	T	K	L	M	P	Y	Q	S

Crusades

The Crusades were wars fought between Christians and Muslims for control of the Holy Lands. Armies of knights traveled thousands of miles across Europe attempting to capture Jerusalem. Between the years 1095 and 1270 there were 7 major Crusades.

Help this knight find his way out of Jerusalem, home to his castle.

Captured!

A captured knight was often thrown into a dungeon to wait for someone to pay his ransom. Ordinary criminals were not so lucky. They were usually punished by fine or execution.

Help the captured knight find his way out of the castle dungeon to freedom.

FINISH

START

Castle

A castle is a fortress made of stone, built to protect a knight and his followers from their enemies.

Hidden in the puzzle are words that describe parts of a castle. Read the definitions below. Then, find and circle the words in the puzzle.

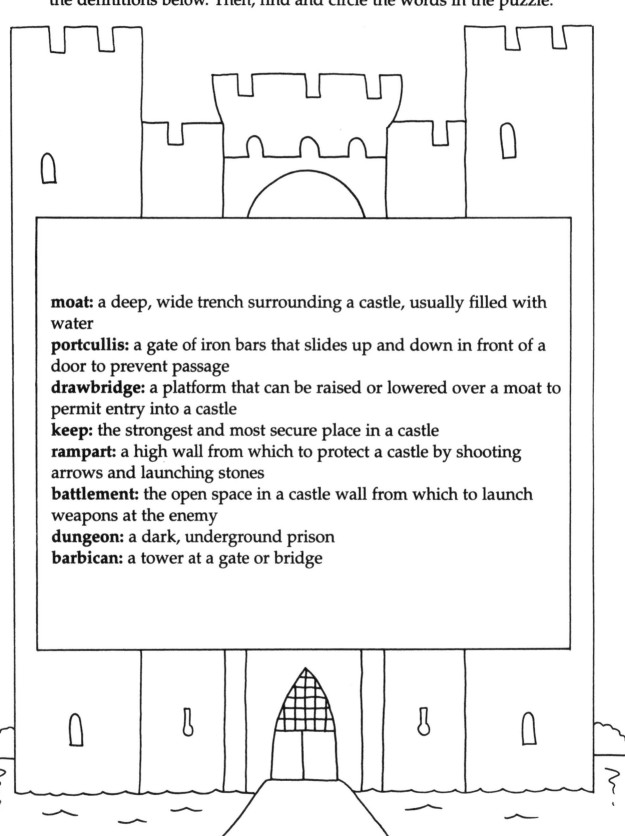

moat: a deep, wide trench surrounding a castle, usually filled with water

portcullis: a gate of iron bars that slides up and down in front of a door to prevent passage

drawbridge: a platform that can be raised or lowered over a moat to permit entry into a castle

keep: the strongest and most secure place in a castle

rampart: a high wall from which to protect a castle by shooting arrows and launching stones

battlement: the open space in a castle wall from which to launch weapons at the enemy

dungeon: a dark, underground prison

barbican: a tower at a gate or bridge

C	R	F	T	Z	O	L	B	Q	A	P	D	F
B	A	T	T	L	E	M	E	N	T	S	U	R
E	M	G	J	N	R	V	X	A	E	F	N	L
Y	P	O	R	T	C	U	L	L	I	S	G	I
G	A	Z	B	A	R	B	I	C	A	N	E	B
H	R	J	N	O	P	T	U	V	W	A	O	D
K	T	Q	S	C	D	U	F	H	I	L	N	H
L	S	E	G	J	K	M	P	Q	Z	X	I	K
M	R	N	D	R	A	W	B	R	I	D	G	E
R	A	S	V	U	B	T	C	D	F	H	J	E
G	J	L	W	M	O	A	T	N	Q	U	K	P

The Castle at Peace

The castle was the knight's home, but other people lived there too. The most important room in the castle was used by everyone for eating, conducting business, and even sleeping.

To find out the name of this room, cross out the letters F, B, Q, and C in the puzzle in the tapestry. Write the remaining letters from each row in the spaces below.

Eating

Mealtimes in a medieval castle were different from mealtimes at home today. In a castle, people sat together on long benches and drank weak ale, even for breakfast. People ate from pieces of bread instead of from plates. They dipped their fingers into large bowls of stew.

Use the code to find out why people ate with their hands. The first letter is done for you.

a	=	Q	n	=	K
b	=	D	o	=	A
c	=	Z	p	=	Y
d	=	M	q	=	I
e	=	U	r	=	X
f	=	C	s	=	B
g	=	R	t	=	H
h	=	L	u	=	P
i	=	S	v	=	G
j	=	E	w	=	O
k	=	N	x	=	J
l	=	V	y	=	F
m	=	T	z	=	W

___ ___ ___ ___ ___
m t j g j

___ ___ ___ ___
z j g j

___ ___
k w

___ ___ ___ ___ ___ !
y w g n i

25

Manors and Towns

When a knight was given land in **return for service**, he became Lord of the Manor. The villagers nearby **were required** to furnish food for the knight and his household. **In return, he** protected them from enemy attacks.

To see what kind of food a typical **villager might** have provided for the manor house, fill in the crossword puzzle below.

Entertainment

Life in a castle could be fun. People played board games, and listened to traveling musicians and storytellers. Sometimes a knight would employ a clown to live in his castle; sometimes a local person would dress up in a costume and perform.

To find out the name of the clown, start at arrow number 1. Go around the circle in the direction of the arrow. Write down every other letter in the space below.

To learn the name of the person in the costume, do the same as before, beginning at arrow number two.

1. ___ ___ ___ ___ ___

2. ___ ___ ___ ___ ___ ___

Decline of the Knights

By the early 16th century, knights were losing importance. Countries began to rely on professional armies. Guns could pierce the strongest armor; cannons made short work of even the stoutest castle walls. But the lore and legends of knights live on.

To find out the name of the most famous group of knights, solve the puzzle. We have filled in the first letter for you.

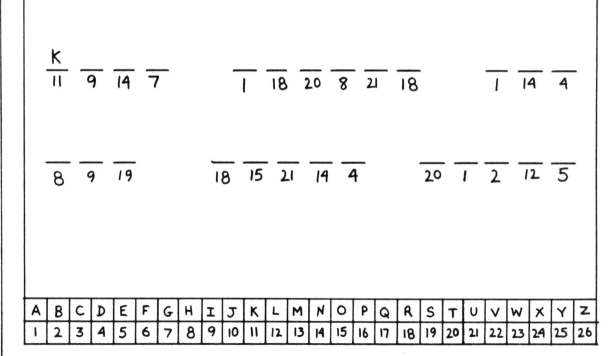

$$\frac{K}{11}\ \frac{}{9}\ \frac{}{14}\ \frac{}{7} \qquad \frac{}{1}\ \frac{}{18}\ \frac{}{20}\ \frac{}{8}\ \frac{}{21}\ \frac{}{18} \qquad \frac{}{1}\ \frac{}{14}\ \frac{}{4}$$

$$\frac{}{8}\ \frac{}{9}\ \frac{}{19} \qquad \frac{}{18}\ \frac{}{15}\ \frac{}{21}\ \frac{}{14}\ \frac{}{4} \qquad \frac{}{20}\ \frac{}{1}\ \frac{}{2}\ \frac{}{12}\ \frac{}{5}$$

A	B	C	D	E	F	G	H	I	J	K	L	M	N	O	P	Q	R	S	T	U	V	W	X	Y	Z
1	2	3	4	5	6	7	8	9	10	11	12	13	14	15	16	17	18	19	20	21	22	23	24	25	26

Solutions

page 1

page 2

(ANSWERS, IN PART) MAD, MADE, DIM, DIME, SLIM, SLIME,
SAG, SAGE, GAS, SAG, DIG, DID, DAD, LAD, LID, LIME, SAD,
SADDLE, LED, LEAD, SLED, SLID, ME, MEAD, MELD, MILD, SEED,
MEDDLE, MEDAL, FLAG, LAG, LEG, GAL, GEL, IS, AS, DEED,
DEAD, GILD, GLIDE, IDLE, GLEAM, GAME, LAME, SAME

page 3

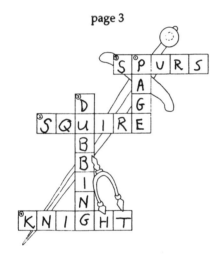

page 4

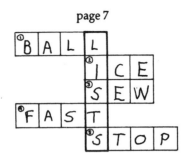

PEL

page 5

QUINTAIN

page 6

CLUB TOURNEY

page 7

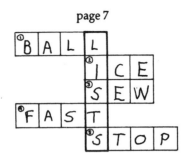

B	A	L	L
			I	C	E
			S	E	W
F	A	S	T	
			T	
			S	T	O	P

page 8

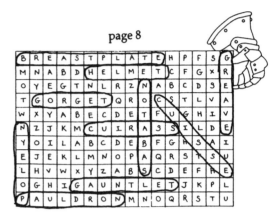

page 10

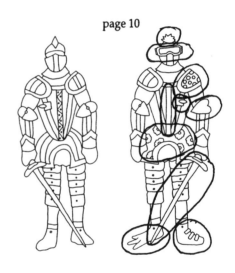

page 11

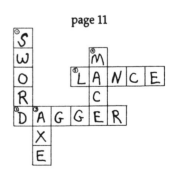

page 13

DESTRIER, PALFREY, SUMPTER, HACKNEY

page 16

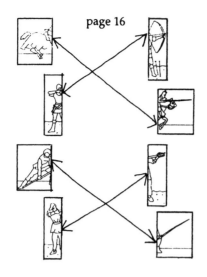

page 17

page 18

B	D	G	N	I	N	I	M	F	G
C	A	T	A	P	U	L	T	H	J
K	L	R	M	O	Q	P	R	S	T
N	E	E	U	B	C	D	E	F	G
X	N	B	A	L	L	I	S	T	A
Y	O	U	E	H	I	J	K	L	M
S	G	C	Z	L	R	Q	P	O	N
T	N	H	U	V	F	W	X	A	B
C	A	E	D	E	F	R	G	Z	H
I	M	T	K	L	M	P	Y	Q	S

page 19

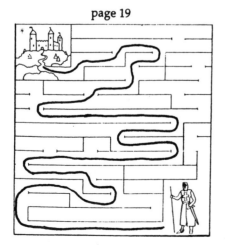

pages 20–21

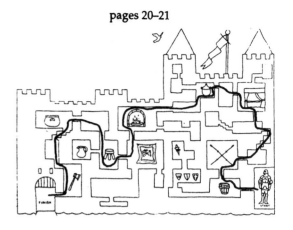

page 23

C	R	F	T	Z	O	L	B	Q	A	P	D	F
B	A	T	T	L	E	M	E	N	T	S	U	R
E	M	G	J	N	R	V	X	A	E	F	N	L
Y	P	O	R	T	C	U	L	L	I	S	G	I
G	A	Z	B	A	R	B	I	C	A	N	E	B
H	R	J	N	O	P	T	U	V	W	A	O	D
K	T	Q	S	C	D	U	F	H	I	L	N	H
L	S	E	G	J	K	M	P	Q	Z	X	I	K
M	R	N	D	R	A	W	B	R	I	D	G	E
R	A	S	V	U	B	T	C	D	F	H	J	E
G	J	L	W	M	O	A	T	N	Q	U	K	P

page 24

GREAT HALL

page 25

THERE WERE NO FORKS

page 26

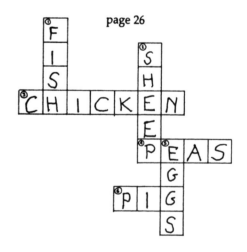

page 27

JESTER, MUMMER

page 28

KING ARTHUR AND HIS ROUND TABLE